Be A Strong And Tall Tree

Jonathan Savage

Hog Press
an imprint of Culicidae Press
PO Box 620647
Middleton, WI 53562-0647
USA
hogpress.com
editor@hogpress.com
+1 (352) 388-3848
+1 (515) 462-0278

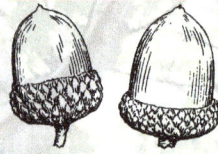

Be A Strong And Tall Tree
2023 © Jonathan Savage

ISBN: 978-1-941892-69-5

Our books may be purchased in bulk for promotional, educational or business use. Please contact your local bookseller or the Hog Press Sales Department at +1-515-462-0278 or email us at sales@hogpress.com

twitter.com/culicidaepress – facebook.com/culicidaepress

Book layout and design by polytekton ©2023, based on a design by Lisa Hovis.

ALL PHOTOGRAPHS BY THE AUTHOR.

For my precious daughters
Whitney, Lesley and Jordan,
their husbands and children,
and my nephews and nieces,
and their families.

I ask that you always live strong, stand tall, be happy and well,
be productive, stay alert (for negative actions as well as positive
opportunities), be humbly and habitually compassionate to ALL
others, and, believe and practice the message of this little book
that God gave me the opportunity to put together for you.
I have always loved you, more
than I love my own life (which I dearly do).

With all respect and love to you,

Dad, Father-in-Law,
Grandfather (Aapah) and Uncle

October 2023

I see all of us as trees planted by the hand of God the Father, Who is our Creator, Father and Source of life.

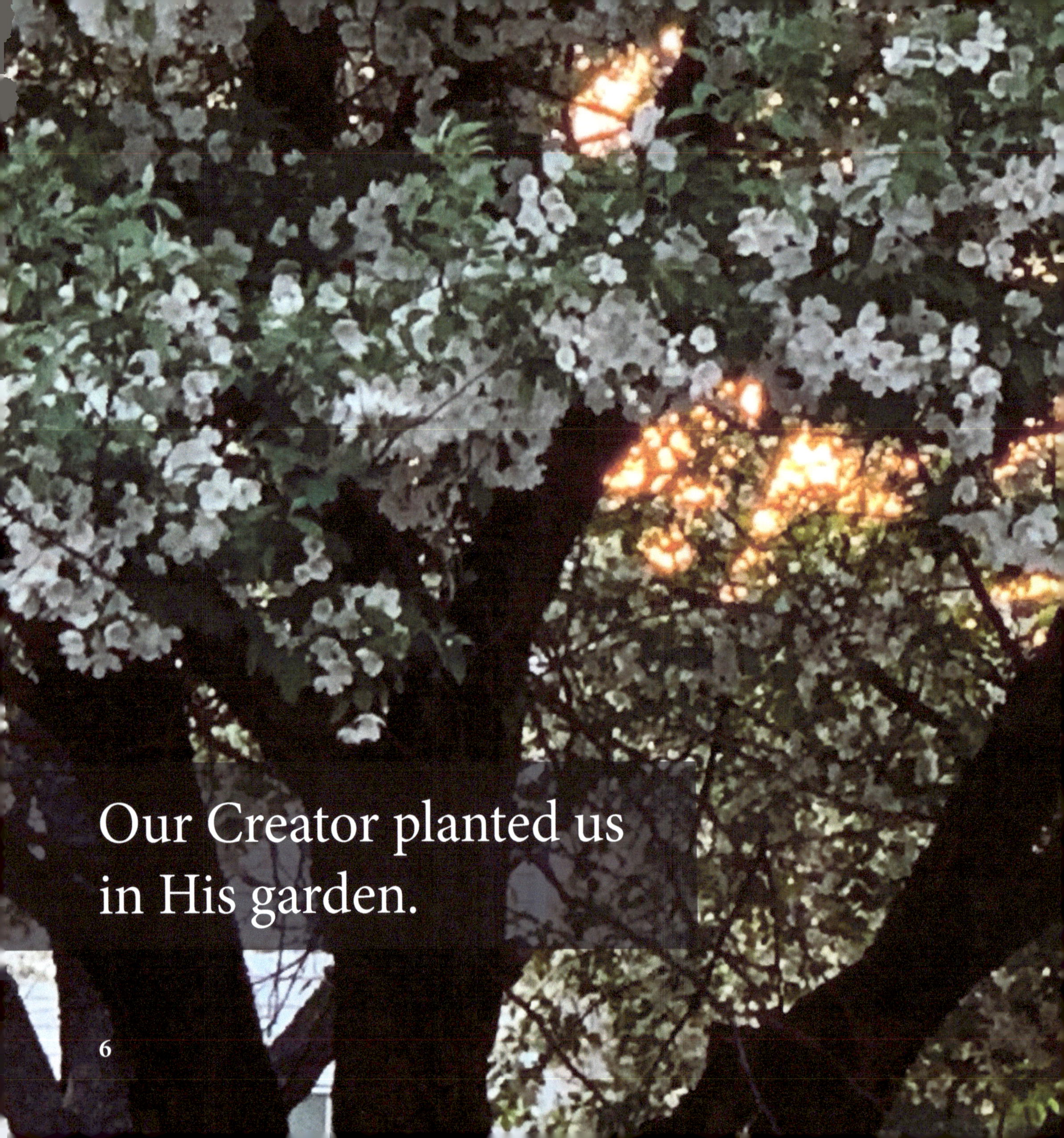

Our Creator planted us
in His garden.

We are all trees — strong, tall, productive, visible and planted by streams of water. And, because of Jesus Christ's sacrificial love, by dying on the cross for our sins (uniquely awful and slow way to be made to suffer and eventually die), and our acceptance and belief in the risen Jesus Christ as our Lord and Savior, God the Holy Spirit is our stream of Living Water, flowing through us to —

Quench our thirst,
Nourish our body,
Revive our soul, and
Give us wisdom and
direction.

"Blessed is the man that walketh not in the counsel of the ungodly, nor standeth in the way of sinners, nor sitteth in the seat of the scornful. But his delight is in the law of the Lord; and in His law doth he meditate day and night. And he shall be like a tree planted by the rivers of water, that bringeth forth his fruit in his season; his leaf also shall not wither; and whatsoever he doeth shall prosper. The ungodly are not so: but are like the chaff which the wind driveth away. Therefore, the ungodly shall not stand in the judgment, nor sinners in the congregation of the righteous. For the Lord knoweth the way of the righteous: but the way of the ungodly shall perish." Psalms 1:1-6 King James Bible

"If any man thirst, let him come unto Me, and drink." St John 7:37b King James Bible

"I am the vine, ye are the branches: He that abideth in Me, and I in him, the same bringeth forth much fruit: for without Me ye can do nothing."
John 15:5 King James Bible

"Thus sayeth the Lord; Cursed be the man that trusteth in man, and maketh flesh his arm, and whose heart departeth from the Lord. For he shall be like heath in the desert, and shall not see when good cometh; but shall inhabit the parched places in the wilderness, in a salt land and not inhabited. Blessed is the man that trusteth in the Lord, and whose hope the Lord is. For he shall be as a tree planted by the waters, that spreadeth out her roots by the river, and shall not see when heat cometh, but her leaf shall be green, and shall not be careful in the year of drought, neither shall cease from yielding fruit."
Jeremiah 17:5-8 King James Bible

Only by stretching your roots to drink the Living Water, which Living Water symbolizes our constant and deliberate relationship with the Triune God, being God the Father, God the Son (Jesus Christ), and God the Holy Spirit, will you ever find…

truth, wisdom, perfect instruction, deep and long-lasting happiness and most importantly — eternal life.

"For God so loved the world, that He gave His only begotten Son, that whosoever believeth in Him should not perish, but have everlasting life."

St John 3:16 -King James Bible

"And the peace of God, which passeth all understanding, shall keep your hearts and minds through Christ Jesus."
— Philippians 4:7 -King James Bible

"God is our refuge and strength, a very present help in trouble."
— Psalms 46:1
-King James Bible

I have always loved trees,
And I tried to draw pictures of them as a little boy,
And had them framed for my parents and grandparents.

As I grew older, I saw trees as a symbol
Of my relationship with God.
Here I try to share with you
An analogy to my life
As a tree created by, cared for and living for
God the Father, God the Son (Jesus Christ),
and God the Holy Spirit.

Jonathan Savage